Mahler's Con

Ronald Harwood's plays include *The Dresser*,
Another Time, *Taking Sides* and *Quartet*. He is also
the author of *Sir Donald Wolfit, CBE: His Life and
Work in the Unfashionable Theatre*, and a history of
theatre, *All the World's a Stage*. He is the editor
of *The Faber Book of Theatre*. He was Visitor in
Theatre at Balliol College, Oxford, was President
of English PEN from 1990 to 1993, and President
of International PEN from 1993 to 1997. In 2000 he
was awarded the Stefan Mitrov Ljubisa Prize for his
contribution to European literature and human rights.
He was elected Chairman of the Royal Society of
Literature in 2001. In 1996 he was appointed Chevalier
de l'Ordre des Arts et des Lettres, and in 1999 he was
awarded a CBE.

RONALD HARWOOD

Mahler's Conversion

faber and faber

First published in 2001
by Faber and Faber Limited
3 Queen Square, London WC1N 3AU
Published in the United States by Faber and Faber Inc.
an affiliate of Farrar, Straus and Giroux LLC, New York

Typeset by Country Setting, Kingsdown, Kent CT14 8ES
Printed by CPI Antony Rowe, Eastbourne

The right of Ronald Harwood to be identified as author
of this work has been asserted in accordance with Section 77
of the Copyright, Designs and Patents Act 1988

A CIP record for this book
is available from the British Library

ISBN 978–0–571–21231–6

2 4 6 8 10 9 7 5 3 1

For Humphrey Burton

Mahler's Conversion was presented by David Aukin for Act Productions and had its first performance at the Yvonne Arnaud Theatre, Guildford, on 5 September 2001, and subsequently opened at the Aldwych Theatre, London, on 17 September 2001. The cast was as follows:

Gustav Mahler Antony Sher
Natalie Bauer-Lechner Alexandra Mathie
Anna von Mildenburg Anna Francolini
Siegfried Lipiner Nickolas Grace
Father Swider/Sigmund Freud Gary Waldhorn
Alma Schindler Fiona Glascott

Directed by Gregory Doran
Designed by Stephen Brimson Lewis
Lighting by Tim Mitchell
Sound by John A. Leonard for Aura

Characters

Gustav Mahler

Natalie Bauer-Lechner

Anna von Mildenburg

Siegfried Lipiner

Father Swider / Sigmund Freud

Alma Schindler

*The action takes place at various times
in various places, beginning in Hamburg in 1897
and ending in Vienna in 1911*

MAHLER'S CONVERSION

Act One

A soprano singing Lob des hohen Verstandes *to piano accompaniment.*
Hamburg. Hotel suite, 1897.
Morning. Siegfried Lipiner and Natalie Bauer-Lechner.
Siegfried is fortyish, gnome-like. Natalie, aged 39, is dressed in male clothing and lies full-stretch, her face covered by a top hat. For the moment, she looks like a man. Prominent, a capacious handbag.
They are waiting patiently, listening to the song.
The song breaks off abruptly.

A Woman's Voice Stop that, you'll tear it, oh God, you're a caveman! Wait! You have to wait!

A Man's Voice I can't wait! I never wait!

The sound of something falling – a chair perhaps. Then:
A glorious young woman, Anna von Mildenburg, aged 24, bursts in. She is in disarray, her bodice open. She sees Siegfried and Natalie, stops dead, gives a little scream, covers herself, runs off, returns a second later, grabs the capacious handbag and disappears again.
Siegfried is impressed by her and smiles. Natalie has momentarily removed her top hat to see what's going on.
After a moment, Gustav Mahler, aged 37, emerges from the bedroom. He is nervy, charged,

3

intense. He is now angry. He is dressed untidily, his hair a mess. He walks in a curious way, abruptly changing the rhythm of his step. He is putting on his jacket.

Mahler I thought I put 'Do Not Disturb' on the door.

Siegfried chuckles.

Natalie We called your name but you didn't answer. (*to Siegfried*) We should've waited downstairs, I told you we should've waited downstairs –

Mahler You said you wouldn't be arriving in Hamburg until this afternoon. Who let you in?

Natalie The chambermaid.

Mahler This isn't a hotel, it's a brothel.

Siegfried laughs loudly.

We were rehearsing.

Siegfried Rehearsing what? (*He becomes helpless.*)

Mahler All right, all right, thank you, joke's over, thank you. (*Paces, stops, paces, stops.*) Well?

Siegfried (*trying to stop laughing*) Well, well, well.

Natalie sits up and shakes free her hair.

Natalie Not well.

Mahler What's that mean?

Awkward pause.

Natalie Some progress but not much.

Mahler Tell me.

Siegfried and Natalie speak at the same time:

Siegfried I talked to Karpath who, of course, being a journalist –

Natalie But there is one ray of hope, Prince Montenuovo is your ally –

They stop. Natalie gestures with exaggerated politeness to allow Siegfried to continue. After a moment's thought:

Siegfried Vienna, in this year of their Lord, 1897, is a city that makes Byzantium seem like a Trappist monastery. The buzzing, the hissing, the whispers are absolutely deafening. Intrigue has as usual replaced coffee as the city's favourite beverage. Instead of mocha, waiters say Mahler. The only question on everyone's lips is, 'Will they appoint a Jew to the Court Opera?' According to Karpath – and he, after all, is a journalist and therefore knows everything – you have many allies –

Natalie Especially Prince Montenuovo –

A brief silence.

Mahler But.

Siegfried But. You also have many enemies who will bar your way even if you meet 'the essential condition'.

Natalie The old story.

Mahler They won't have me.

Natalie They won't have you unless.

Siegfried No, no, let's be fair. Not *won't* have you unless. *Can't* have you unless.

Mahler paces, stops.

Mahler (*sudden vehemence*) I'm sick of anti-Semitism.

Siegfried You mustn't be. It is absolutely necessary. It defines you as a Jew.

Unobtrusively, Anna emerges from the bedroom, now dressed.

Mahler I don't want to be defined as a Jew. I want to be defined as a musician. I want to be defined as a human being.

Siegfried (*wincing*) Please don't say things like that. They make me squirm.

Anna Why?

Siegfried rises, bows.

Siegfried (*with some pleasure*) I believe we've already met.

Anna (*smiling, flirtatious*) Yes, but not formally.

Siegfried No, not at all formally.

Mahler Forgive me: Anna von Mildenburg, Siegfried Lipiner. She's the most promising soprano in Europe –

Siegfried Yes, I know – (*kissing her hand*) Dear lady. I am a great admirer of your gifts. I also think you have a beautiful voice.

Anna is amused.

Mahler You know Natalie.

Anna I know Natalie.

Natalie And I know Anna.

Anna (*a false smile*) Welcome to Hamburg, Natalie. (*to Siegfried*) Why does Gustav saying he wants to be defined as a human being make you squirm?

Siegfried Because it puts me in mind of Democritus and his ridiculous aphorism, 'One man means as much to me as a multitude, and a multitude only as much as one man.' It's total nonsense. I prefer our own mad, dear little Friedrich: 'Become thyself.'

Natalie Does Nietzsche say that?

Siegfried He says little else.

Anna (*to Siegfried*) You're too clever for me.

Natalie He's too clever for everyone.

Siegfried Quite true, I'm even too clever for myself. (*to Anna*) I'll send you my collected works. Don't be alarmed, I've only written one book: *Prometheus Unbound*. It's a work of genius. And that's not only the opinion of several dear friends but it's my opinion also. Perhaps you would allow me to –?

Mahler (*interrupting; urgent*) What must I do?

Silence.

Natalie We all know what you must do.

Silence.

Siegfried You shouldn't have lied to Karpath.

Mahler I didn't lie to him, what d'you mean, lie to him?

Siegfried You told him – this is according to Karpath, of course – he says you told him that you'd been baptised in Budapest.

Natalie Did you tell him that?

No response.

Siegfried As I suspected, Karpath, being a journalist, always tells the truth. He says when you were asked to produce your baptismal certificate, it was not forthcoming. Naughty, Gustav. Very naughty. Karpath wasn't best pleased. Nor, I suspect, was God.

Natalie I know a priest, Father Swider, a good man –

Mahler paces. Siegfried rises, blocks his path and stands face to face with him. Mahler stops dead.

Siegfried (*deadly serious*) I must warn you this is a moment of great danger.

Charged silence.

Anna I wish you hadn't said that, it makes me squirm.

Siegfried smiles crookedly.

Mahler Why danger?

Nothing from Siegfried.

You were baptised. Was it a moment of great danger for you?

Still nothing from Siegfried.

Then don't talk such nonsense.

Anna When were you baptised, Herr Lipiner?

Siegfried I can't remember now. Ten, twelve years ago. When my father learned of it, he said Kaddish for me. That's the prayer for the dead. It was all terribly amusing.

8

Anna Were you a practising Jew?

Siegfried I practised but I never quite got the hang of it.

Mahler You were baptised for the same reason as every other Jew is baptised.

Siegfried Not Our Lord. He was a Jew and was baptised, I believe, for rather different reasons.

Mahler Why is it a moment of danger?

Siegfried Later, Gustav, we'll talk privately –

Mahler My ultimate goal is and must remain Vienna. The whole pattern of my future life depends on it. I was an adolescent when I first set foot in Vienna. You can't imagine what that meant – (*Breaks off; awkward silence.*) Tell me exactly: who did you see and what was said? (*He points at Siegfried as though bringing in an instrument during an orchestral performance.*)

Siegfried Why do you always make me feel like a triangle player in the percussion section?

Anna laughs quietly.

Well now, let's think. (*mostly for Anna's benefit*) I should tell you, dear lady, that I have three amazing gifts. One is for self-advertisement. The second is the ability to drop names on a symphonic scale. The third is a supernatural instinct to find my way through a labyrinth of a design more complex than the one said to have been built in Crete by Daedalus. I refer, of course, to the labyrinth known as the Court of His Imperial Catholic Majesty, the Emperor Franz Josef.

Mahler Get on with it, Sigi –

Siegfried My tempi are always too slow for him. I have access to the corridors of impotence because I am, no less, Librarian to the Austrian Parliament. Does that impress you?

Anna Not much.

Siegfried Good. You have discernment. I shall now demonstrate my three gifts perfectly. I called on my good friend, Count Josef von Bezecny, general manager of all court theatres including the opera. Not a liberal but nevertheless an ally. He was delighted to see me, accounting me one of the most intelligent men in Vienna. He is therefore a man of impeccable judgement. I told the dear Count that Gustav's well-known reputation for arrogance and venom was wholly undeserved. I'm not sure he was entirely convinced. So, I followed up with a little letter saying that while Gustav has without doubt a passionate nature he combines it with the greatest self-control and an even almost unbelievable patience.

Mahler laughs.

Yes, I suppose I'd better now cross myself and ask God's forgiveness. (*He crosses himself, puts his hands together and pretends to pray.*)

Mahler (*amused*) You're a good friend.

Siegfried And an even better liar.

Mahler (*pointing*) Natalie.

Natalie I saw Rosa Papier.

Anna Darling Rosa, how is she? The best teacher I ever had.

Mahler Second best.

They laugh softly and intimately.

Natalie She's in rude health. She asked me to deliver these letters. (*Produces two similar envelopes; she hands one to Gustav, the other to Anna.*) She said she's talked to her friend Eduard Wlassack. He told her he was particularly impressed that Brahms supported you.

Siegfried (*for Anna's benefit*) That will be my good friend Johannes Brahms. Another composer.

He chuckles. Anna reads her letter.

Mahler And what's all this about Prince Montenuovo?

Siegfried Dear Alfred Montenuovo, the most disagreeable man in all the Empire –

Natalie Yes, but powerful. And he's reported to have said he admires you, supports you and, if you were appointed, would protect you. But.

Mahler But.

Siegfried But.

Silence while Mahler paces.

There's a very good Jewish joke doing the rounds.

Mahler (*stops pacing, venomous*) I don't want to hear it, I despise Jewish jokes.

Siegfried You won't despise this one. Two poor old Jews, Kahn and Levi, of course, are passing St Stephen's. They see a notice: 'Any Jew who comes into the Cathedral and converts to Catholicism will receive one

thousand florins.' So Kahn decides to enter He's gone
about an hour and then emerges. Levi says, 'Well, did
they convert you?' And Kahn says, 'Certainly.' 'And
are you now a Catholic?' 'That's what I am,' says
Kahn. 'And did they give you the thousand florins?'
And Kahn says, 'That's the trouble with you Jews,
all you think about is money.'

*The others laugh, not Mahler. He paces again, then
suddenly stops. Involuntarily, his right foot beats a
rapid tattoo.*

Mahler I was fifteen when I first set foot in Vienna.
I've never recovered from the shock. I was, still am,
enthralled by Vienna. By its elegance, culture, luxury,
hospitality, its – its – its sensuality –

Anna laughs quietly at something in her letter:

And this above all, the morality of Vienna is tolerance.

*Siegfried laughs; Natalie takes out a small notebook
and makes notes.*

All right, laugh, but you know I'm speaking the truth.
And what other city in the whole world loves music
as much? Vienna sings. Vienna dances. It has its own
tempo, stately, unhurried. Even the trams are
melodious. They clatter by in tune, and moderato.

Siegfried laughs again.

All right, all right, but you can't deny that wherever
you go, at every level of society, be it an archduke or
a street-cleaner, the talk is of music. There are people
still alive who knew Beethoven and Schubert. On any
day of the week I could visit Brahms or Bruckner

Siegfried And you could also sit all day in cafés, buy one cup of coffee, play cards, read newspapers, argue, gossip, intrigue, and waste your life away like every other Viennese. You only have to look at me.

Mahler But it's life, Sigi, life, life, *life*! Just think of the people, their energy, their brilliance, their faces, clothes, accents, their dazzling variety. And you can live in Vienna for years and years and yet one day suddenly discover an alleyway, a street, even a square with great domed buildings filling the sky. And tell me this: where else can you find such delicious apricot dumplings?

They both laugh.

Vienna isn't simply a city, it's a world in itself. I want to be part of it. No. I want to be the centre of it.

Natalie Then you know what you must do. If they appoint you to the Court Opera –

Mahler If, if, if –

Natalie If they appoint you to the Court Opera, they can do so on only one condition.

Silence.

Anna Is it such a big step, Gustl?

Silence.

Siegfried A cousin of mine has just become a Protestant. But then he's not very ambitious.

Mahler Why did you use the word danger?

Siegfried Later.

Mahler Why will it be dangerous? Yes, I'm born a Jew. I went to the synagogue as a child and naturally I sang my bar mitzvah portion like an angel –

Siegfried Naturally –

Mahler But I also sang in the choir of the local Catholic church. In fact, I preferred the local Catholic church because the music was better. Haydn, Beethoven, Mozart's *Requiem*, Rossini's *Stabat Mater*. I felt a part of something then. And now, why am I, what am I, who am I?

Siegfried You are in Hamburg, a Jew, but wanting not to be.

Mahler You have no idea what I'm talking about, do you? I'm talking about my identity as a man, as an artist, as a musician.

Siegfried It's very fashionable to talk of identity just at the moment. I blame Sigmund Freud. My identity has never bothered me. I have to become who I am. That's the difficulty –

Mahler I belong nowhere.

Siegfried You exaggerate –

Mahler I do not!

Siegfried You overdramatise –

Mahler I do not! You just don't hear the discords. I'm isolated. I'm alone. I belong nowhere!

Natalie No, no, you're quite wrong, you belong everywhere!

Distant thunder.

Mahler I do not! I'm homeless. Not once but three times. First, a native of Bohemia in Austria. Second, an Austrian among Germans. And third, a Jew in the rest of the world. Everywhere an intruder. Never welcomed. It's intolerable. I want to find a home. I resent being forced into this unbearable conflict. Why are they doing this to me? It's torture. Why should my being a Jew make a difference? Don't they know, for God's sake, that there's no such thing as a Jewish B-flat?

Distant thunder.

Natalie (*gently*) Gustav my dear, you must decide soon. Otherwise the opportunity will pass and they will appoint someone else.

Mahler Who? There is no one else.

Siegfried You won't believe this but anti-Semites always seem to have a knack of finding someone else.

Natalie Cosima Wagner is said to have recommended Felix Mottl.

Mahler But he can barely keep time –

Siegfried I once had a conversation with Cosima. Shortly after Richard died. She'd been reading a book. By her son-in-law. The title, as I remember, was *Chamberlain's Nineteenth Century*. She said it was a fascinating work because the author explained what distinguishes Semites from Germans. Apparently, Germans have a strong penchant for religion and this penchant is totally lacking in the Jews. Dear Cosima. So true to the family tradition.

Mahler God, we're at the end of the nineteenth century and still enslaved by the most primitive bigotry. Why do they hate us so much?

Thunder nearer.

Siegfried I suspect Jews have been asking that question at the end of every century since the beginning of time.

Mahler My head is throbbing. I need air. Sigi, walk with me –

Siegfried But there's a storm brewing –

Mahler (*to Anna*) I won't be back until late –

Anna You promised to take me out to dinner tonight –

Mahler I've changed my plans.

Anna But I've been looking forward to it all week.

Mahler (*brutally*) I can't help that. I want to hear what Sigi has to say and then I have to decide what to do. (*He goes.*)

Anna (*calling after him*) We all know what you'll do. You'll do what's best for Gustav Mahler –

Siegfried chases after him.

Natalie I must follow them –

Anna Oh yes, don't let him out of your sight, you know how quickly his affections change except when it comes to loving himself.

Natalie (*turning on her*) You're a child, you understand nothing.

Anna I understand more than you think. I've held him in my arms, felt the weight of his body on mine, that's more than you'll ever be able to say –

Natalie Read Rosa's letter!

A clap of thunder rather close.

Anna I have. And I agree with every word. And please don't go out like that. Find a cloak. Cover yourself. And then he might think you're a woman.

Anna goes. Natalie, distressed, runs off. Blackout.

Lakeside.
A violent storm raging.
Mahler and Siegfried enter. Siegfried holds an umbrella over their heads. They battle against the wind and rain, and find inadequate shelter, still cowering under the umbrella.
They have to shout.

Siegfried I wish I loved nature as much as you do. Aren't you terrified?

Mahler Nothing in nature frightens me. This is what I want to capture – thunder, wind, rain, the cries of birds, the world itself, primaeval, raw, savage. God, this is wonderful, inspiring, miraculous. (*to the heavens*) More percussion! More brass! Drown me! Drown me!

He laughs; thunder and lightning; then:

Right. Now. Tell me. Why did you use the word danger?

Siegfried Because of what you may lose.

Mahler What will I lose? Being a Jew means nothing to me.

Siegfried You say that just to reassure yourself.

Thunder and lightning.

It's not true –

Mahler What? I didn't hear –

Another terrific thunder clap.

Siegfried Just imagine that your very being is in some dark and arcane way the product of a million years of –

Another thunder clap but not as close.

What if your creativity will slowly wither? What if the few drops of holy water on the crown of your head drowns your genius?

Nothing from Mahler. They fall silent.
  The storm is moving away. Thunder again, but further off.

Siegfried Gustav, listen carefully to what I have to say. We must never betray who we are.

Silence.

I had the gift to be another Goethe. Well, perhaps not Goethe, but another – (*He runs dry.*)

Mahler Your book was much admired –

Siegfried Admiration doesn't pay the rent. (*lost for a moment*) The drops of holy water tarnished what little talent I had. I haven't published another book. I've hardly written another line. I have an emptiness. Some mornings I wake up and hear my father reciting Kaddish. 'Yit-kadal, v' yit-kadash –'

Distant rumblings.

Mahler The storm's passing. (*He pokes his head out from under the umbrella.*) It's stopped raining.

Siegfried (*lowers the umbrella*) The sun is coming out.

Mahler (*suddenly*) Do you believe in a life hereafter?

Siegfried (*disconcerted*) What?

Mahler Is there a life hereafter?

Siegfried I certainly hope not.

Far distant thunder.

Mahler It's impossible that this world is the be-all and the end-all of existence. Don't you agree?

No response.

'Troubled or still, water is always water. What difference can embodiment or disembodiment make to the Liberated? Whether calm or in tempest, the sameness of the Ocean suffers no change.' Those are the words of an eastern mystic.

Siegfried I didn't think they were yours.

Mahler Do you have a cigar? I'm longing for a cigar.

Siegfried reaches into his pocket and finds a cigar.

Siegfried You worry me, Gustav.

Mahler Why?

Siegfried Your mind darts around like a firecracker. If you get to Vienna, I think you should consult Professor Freud.

Mahler Why do you use these words, danger, betrayal? It's so unlike you –

Siegfried I use them because – (*Breaks off; with difficulty.*) You know what I feel for you.

Brief silence.

If you were genuinely seeking after truth, I'd keep silent. If you had faith, I'd keep silent. But you're about to make a decision for the wrong reasons. A cynical decision. A decision to enhance your career and nothing more. I did exactly the same thing. And look at me.

Mahler And what are the right reasons?

Siegfried Wanting to know what we are, why we are, who we are.

Mahler My music will answer all those questions.

Siegfried I wish you weren't so modest.

Silence.

I long to have faith. You can't imagine how I long for faith.

Mahler Odd you should mention your father. I can't get my own father's face out of my mind. His upper lip is twisted and he's yelling at me.

Siegfried Dr Freud lives in Bergasse. Number nineteen.

Mahler (*laughing*) Now, if I were to be psychoanalysed, I would certainly never write another note of music. There'd be no need. For an artist creation is the cure.

Natalie's Voice (*calling*) Gustav! Siegfried!

Siegfried Ah, Lorelei in a top hat.

Mahler (*calling*) Over here! Over here!

Natalie enters wrapped in a cloak.

Natalie I've been looking everywhere – (*She sits beside Mahler.*) And what have you two naughty boys been talking about?

Siegfried Psychoanalysis.

Natalie Really?

Mahler Sigi's advice seems to be that I should turn my back on Vienna.

Siegfried I never said that. I say you ought to go to Vienna. But go as a Jew. Become thyself. (*He chuckles.*)

Natalie That would be madness. Believe me, Gustav, my ambitions are your ambitions. You must be baptised, you must be, then the whole world is yours for the asking.

Siegfried But just remember. Jehovah is the God of vengeance.

Silence.

Mahler I need to make sure.

Natalie Of what?

Mahler If I'm baptised I have to be certain that they'll offer me the job.

Siegfried In Vienna there are no certainties. Just like life, Gustav, life, life, life.

Silence.

Mahler (*with great force*) My time will come!

Silence.

Natalie There's something else.

Mahler What?

Natalie Have you read Rosa's letter yet?

Mahler No, I haven't even opened it.

Natalie Read it.

Mahler Why? Do you know what's in it?

Natalie She told me she's given you some important advice. Concerning – (*She breaks off.*)

Awkward silence.

Mahler Concerning?

She summons courage.

Natalie Anna von Mildenburg.

Siegfried Ah, she with two breasts of heavenly sheen. Does she often walk about like that or was it just my lucky day?

Mahler What about Anna?

Natalie Read Rosa's letter.

Mahler searches for and finds the envelope, tears it open, reads. They watch him. He stands suddenly.

Mahler Find me a priest.

Blackout.

Hamburg. Hotel suite.
From the darkness:

Father Swider's Voice (*calling*) Dr Mahler? Dr Mahler?

The light grows to reveal Father Swider, an apparently confident man, in his fifties. He carries a briefcase.

Father Swider (*calling again*) Dr Mahler –?

He waits. After a moment, Mahler enters. He has just woken from a nap.

Mahler Yes?

Father Swider Ah, Dr Mahler. I am Father Swider. Our mutual friend, Natalie –

Mahler Yes, yes, of course, I am sorry to have kept you waiting. I've been rehearsing all morning. I always take a nap and I dream so vividly in the afternoons –

Father Swider Please don't apologise. There really is no need. (*He stares hard at Mahler.*) This is a glorious day for the Church.

Mahler gazes into space.

I am a great admirer of your music. (*Takes out a small book, the Catechism.*) I have heard your First Symphony and many of your songs. But it is your Second Symphony which is most inspiring. The one you call 'Resurrection'.

Mahler paces.

Allow me, as a lover of music, an amateur, of course, allow me to say that I consider you to be one of the musical giants of our age. I always defend you against your critics. I am honoured to be here in your presence. But I have to confess, I have also a personal favour to ask of you. However, all in good –

Mahler suddenly kneels in front of the priest.

Dr Mahler, are you not well?

Mahler I'm ready for baptism. I thought it appropriate to kneel.

Father Swider But I haven't come to baptise you.

Mahler I thought it was understood –

Father Swider What was understood?

Mahler That I wanted to be baptised into the Catholic Church –

Father Swider Yes, yes, yes, of course I know that –

Mahler Well then, let's get on with it –

Father Swider It's not as straightforward as that.

Mahler Why not?

Father Swider I have certain questions to ask about your intentions, your motives, and I must ascertain what progress you have made with the Catechism. Natalie, I hope, gave you the –

Mahler I have done my best with the Catechism but I have a very bad memory –

Father Swider Really? I thought as a musician –

Mahler Yes, for music, yes, music, but for other things. I have to carry a notebook, write down everything in case I forget –

Father Swider Nevertheless, I really must discover what progress you have made –

Mahler Is it not possible to be baptised first and then afterwards to learn the Catechism? I was told it was perfectly usual, acceptable, common practice, baptism first, then –

Father Swider It's certainly possible but as a priest I have sacred responsibilities in these matters, I have to –

He runs dry. Mahler gazes at him. He stands.

Mahler Yes, of course. You must forgive me, Father. I am an impatient man. The truth is I'm rather frightened and anxious –

Father Swider The truth is, Dr Mahler, so am I. I have converted many people: Lutherans, an Orthodox priest and even two Muslims. But I have never before converted a Jew. And never anyone so – You will be my first Jew. I regard it as an honour.

Mahler Ask what you have to ask.

Father Swider You are a Jew by birth?

Mahler There is no other way of being a Jew, Father.

Father Swider Yes, yes, but was your mother a Jewess? Because, as you surely know but as I have only recently found out, according to your ancient Talmudic law, it is if the mother is Jewish –

Mahler My mother was a Jewess. Her maiden name was Hermann. Maria Hermann.

Father Swider Maria. Good.

Mahler She was gentleness itself. My father was not gentle. He had a violent temper. He made cheap liqueurs.

Father Swider Are they still alive?

Mahler No.

Father Swider And may I ask your reasons for wanting to become a Catholic?

Mahler Was all this not explained to you?

Father Swider No. I'm afraid not. So, I should like to know have you, over the years, from childhood perhaps, been in search of the truth which has finally led you to our Lord Jesus Christ? Your 'Resurrection' Symphony seems to suggest that was the path you followed.

Mahler hesitates.

Mahler Not exactly.

Father Swider Excellent. Then it must have been a sudden moment of inspiration, like St Paul blinded on the road to Damascus.

Mahler hesitates again.

Mahler Not exactly.

Father Swider What then?

Mahler I want to be honest with you, Father.

Father Swider I very much hope so.

After a moment:

Mahler There is a movement afoot to have me appointed to the Court Opera in Vienna.

Father Swider Splendid, congratulations – (*then, realising*) Oh, I see.

Mahler It is likely that first I will be invited only as a conductor, and later, be confirmed as director. I have no guarantees but as you know better than I, such a position can only be filled by a Catholic.

Father Swider Dr Mahler, this is not a good reason for conversion.

Mahler I have religious longings, Father.

Father Swider But to want to become a Catholic in order simply to be appointed –

Mahler (*flaring*) Simply? Simply? There's nothing simple about it. It's a – a – plague. I'm trying to rid myself of an infection.

Father Swider Yes, I understand that, I understand that being a Jew must feel –

Mahler No, not my infection, theirs. True, I have never been much of a Jew. But when I was eight years old, my favourite brother, Ernst, died. It was a terrible time. Shortly afterwards, I had a dream that still haunts me. In the dream, my mother, Ernst and I were standing at the window of our apartment. Mother suddenly cried out, 'God, what's happening?' The sky filled with a sulphurous fog. Yellow, choking, apocalyptic. Then, as is the way with dreams, I found myself in the marketplace and through the vapour swirling about me, I glimpsed a figure, the terrifying figure of the Eternal Jew. There was a wind which made his coat billow so that he looked like a hunchback. But there was something else about him, something astonishing. He was carrying a gnarled, twisted staff and on the top was a golden cross. Yes, a golden cross. He began to chase after me, trying to give me this staff, this staff crowned with the golden cross, but at that moment I woke up and cried out. I've always believed that the dream was a warning to me that I, too, would become a restless wanderer, not in the literal sense, but spiritually. And soon after that dream someone asked me what I wanted to be, and I said, 'I want to be a martyr.' I know those were the words of a child but I don't want to be a martyr, Father. I don't want to be spiritually restless. I want a home. I want to find my own still centre.

Silence. Mahler stares into space.

Father Swider I wonder if I could recommend another priest. There is a man in Vienna who does nothing but convert Jews, rather quickly, I believe –

Mahler Father, may I ask you a question?

No response.

Do you believe, do you honestly and sincerely believe in the life hereafter?

Silence. Father Swider is deeply uncomfortable.

Father Swider I'm not sure of this priest's exact whereabouts, but that's easily found out. Would you like me to put you in touch with him? He is, I seem to remember, a Jesuit.

Mahler Don't you ever have doubts, profound, disturbing doubts? Help me, Father.

Silence.

Father Swider I will do my best for you, Dr Mahler. But you must do your best for me. And for God.

Mahler I will do what I can.

Father Swider The questions I shall ask may seem to you very silly and primitive but nevertheless I have to ask them.

Mahler Ask.

Father Swider As a Jew, I know you believe in God but –

Mahler As a Jew you do not have to believe in God.

Father Swider What?

Mahler Being a Jew is not conditional on belief in God. You are either a Jew or you are not a Jew. Belief in God is not the membership fee.

Father Swider (*deeply worried*) Are you sure?

No response.

I had no idea. But you do believe. Don't you?

Mahler Believe what?

Father Swider In God.

Mahler Do I believe in God? Let me put it this way.
I find it difficult not to believe in God. I believe in
nature. I believe in philosophy and physics and
metaphysics. I am intrigued by eastern mysticism.
I am not sure that any faith has a monopoly of truth –

Father Swider puts a hand to his head as if in pain.

– but I have a sense of the Creator, of a force so
immense and powerful that it's beyond imagination
and sometimes, no always, beyond understanding,
and it's coming to grips with that force, struggling to
be at one with that creative savagery, which is
represented in every note of music I write. Have you
ever looked at a neglected garden? Have you ever
seen what nature does to man's efforts to defy chaos?
To bring order to ruin and confusion is at the very
heart of creation. To believe that it is possible to
harness the tornado is at the very heart of faith. (*He
is momentarily lost again.*) Today, I glanced again at
the Scherzo of my Second Symphony, yes, yes, the
one I call 'Resurrection'. I haven't looked at it since
I wrote it. I was surprised by it. I asked myself did
I really compose this? It's remarkable, awesome.
It's a great piece but I hadn't thought so while I was
working on it. Creation is a mystical process from
beginning to end. Unconsciously, as if you're in the
grip of a command from outside yourself, you're
compelled to create something you can scarcely
comprehend afterwards. And even more strangely,

this unconscious, mysterious power manifests itself in individual passages and precisely in the most difficult and significant ones. Usually they're the passages I don't want to come to grips with, the ones I want to avoid, the ones which hold me up yet finally demand to be expressed. I can only describe what happens, I can't explain it. It's a force, you see. Outside myself. (*He's lost again.*) You said you had a favour to ask of me.

Father Swider Yes, but not now, perhaps at a –

Anna, wearing a hat and in her street clothes, bursts in, furious. But, seeing the priest, controls herself.

Mahler (*dangerously angry*) I'm in a meeting.

Anna fumes but doesn't move.

Father Swider No, no, I'll go, we'll talk further –

Mahler May I introduce Anna von Mildenburg? Father Swider.

Father Swider My child –

Anna Be careful, Father. He's not to be trusted.

She storms off. Agonising pause.

Mahler I apologise. She's a soprano.

Brief silence.

Father Swider I will be frank with you, Dr Mahler. I am troubled. Not by the young lady, certainly not, that is evidently a private matter, no business of mine. No, I am troubled by our interview. I am uncertain. Forgive me for saying this, but you alarm me. I have

never been in the presence of so – so – (*Breaks off.*)
I will pray for guidance. And I will ask advice from
my Bishop.

Mahler How long will that take?

Father Swider I will have to make an appointment to
see him; a few days, perhaps, a week at most –

Mahler Don't let it be too long, Father. The world
won't wait for me.

Father Swider No, no, no, no.

Silence.

I could make enquiries about this other priest, the one
I mentioned, the Jesuit in Vienna –

Mahler No, Father. There isn't time. I must be baptised
here in Hamburg. When, if I return to Vienna, I must
return a Catholic.

Father Swider nods sadly.

Please help me, Father. I will be eternally grateful.
(*Smiles crookedly.*) Eternally.

*Father Swider leaves quickly. Mahler closes his eyes,
breathes deeply, trying to control his anger.*

Mahler (*calling*) Anna!

No response.

Anna!

Anna re-enters, pushes past him, still seething.

How dare you behave like that.

Anna Why did you ignore me at rehearsal?

Overlapping:

Mahler How dare you say to that priest I'm not to be trusted?

Anna Why did you humiliate me this morning?

Mahler Not now, Anna, I'm not in the mood –

Anna But I am.

Mahler subsides.

Today at the theatre you greeted everyone else, even members of the chorus, you never said a word to me –

Mahler Nonsense, you're too sensitive –

Anna (*continuing, unstoppable*) – never looked at me, not once, never gave me a single direction even when I deliberately sang flat. Why?

Mahler (*exasperated*) Oh for God's sake, you know why.

Anna Yes, I know why, because you're a coward, that's why –

Mahler You want to know, you really want to know?

Anna Yes, I want to know –

Mahler Because you talk too much.

Anna I do what?

Mahler You heard. I said at the beginning our affair has to remain a secret for both our sakes –

Anna Yes, because what really worries you is not that people know about us here in Hamburg but that there's already talk about us in Vienna. Isn't that the truth? They know about us in Vienna and that frightens you, the gossip frightens you –

Mahler That's not true –

Anna Liar! Jewish liar!

She slaps him hard across the face. He slaps her back, then tries to embrace her. She pushes him away.

Anna Don't try that on me, I've seen those operettas, slap, slap, slap and then a loving kiss, cheap theatrical rubbish –

Long silence. They stare at each other.

Mahler I love you, Anna.

Anna Do you? (*Turns to him.*) I'm sorry, I shouldn't have said – I shouldn't have –

Mahler Don't reproach yourself for anything. You're without blame. Just say that you love me.

Anna I love you.

Silence.

But you terrify me. You're utterly ruthless. Your ambition means more to you than I do.

Mahler For God's sake, all I ask is that we be prudent. You think that's easy for me? It's not easy for me. You think that every moment I see you in rehearsal, or when I sit beside you in a café, you think I don't want to embrace you, hold you, kiss you, enter you?

Anna Stop it –

Mahler If we give the slightest reason for further gossip, my position would become even more untenable than it is –

Anna Yes, there you are, you see?

Mahler But you'll suffer, too. You want to sing in Vienna. I want you to sing in Vienna. You think I could engage you if everyone thought I was merely engaging my mistress?

Anna Oh, you're doing this for my sake, are you? I see, I see –

Mahler Shall I read you what Rosa Papier wrote to me?

Anna If you wish.

He takes out the letter.

Mahler (*reads*) 'Beg Anna to be reasonable and not to claim that you compromised her. It was her fault that she chose to advertise the affair in her usual way –

Anna Let me look –

She tries to snatch the letter but he holds on to it and goes on reading.

Mahler 'If you are to see each other in Vienna as often as you do now in Hamburg, you will not be given jobs, either of you. Vienna has rules which only Vienna understands.'

Silence. Anna takes out her letter.

Anna (*reads*) 'For the two of you to marry would be calamitous, absurd, idiotic, sheer folly! Don't you realise that the poor man is suffering as a result of his foolishness? Don't you understand that, like all men, he is weak?'

Silence. Mahler exits slowly.
The beginning of the third movement, 'In ruhig fliessender Bewegung', from the 'Resurrection' Symphony.
Blackout.

The hotel suite.
In darkness.

Father Swider 'Who made you?'

Mahler 'God.'

Father Swider 'Why did he make you?'

Lights on Father Swider and Mahler, both with copies of the Catechism.

Mahler (*glancing at his copy surreptitiously*) 'That I might know him, love him, and serve him in this world, and be happy with him for ever in the next.'

Father Swider Good, good. Your memory is much better than you think.

Mahler Are you frightened of death, Father?

Father Swider Why should one be frightened of death?

Silence.

Mahler There are things that puzzle me.

Father Swider Yes, I am sure. There are things that puzzle us all. Let me try to help.

Mahler (*turning to the page*) For example, these questions: 'Where is God?'

Father Swider Everywhere. Is that puzzling, Dr Mahler?

Mahler And: 'What is mortal sin?'

Father Swider Mortal sin is that which kills the soul and deserves hell.

Mahler Yes, yes, yes, but – (*Reads, paces.*) 'How does mortal sin kill the soul?'

Father Swider 'By destroying the life of the soul, which is the grace of God.' Dr Mahler, I'm supposed to be asking the questions.

Mahler continues to pace.

And I wonder if you would mind sitting down? I have the distinct impression that you're making God very nervous.

Mahler sits.

Mahler I'm sorry. But I'm coming to the crux of it now, the twelfth article of the Creed? 'Life everlasting.'

Father Swider But why should this be puzzling? The catechism asks, 'What means life everlasting?' How do you answer that, Dr Mahler?

Silence.

Life everlasting means that the good shall live for ever happy in heaven. What could be simpler than that?

Mahler I have a terror of death, Father. I can't conceive of a world without me in it. I can't bear to contemplate eternity. I can't imagine oblivion. I can't envisage endless silence. I want at least one note of my music to echo in the void for ever. For ever.

Father Swider Believe in our Lord Jesus Christ and all these terrors will be banished.

Silence.

Mahler Baptise me. I need to be cleansed.

Long silence.

Father Swider One favour deserves another.

Mahler is puzzled.

You may remember at our first meeting I said I had a favour to ask of you? (*Takes papers from his briefcase.*) I myself – I myself compose. I have brought along my setting of *Veni, Creator*. Would you look at it and give me your opinion? I, too, would be eternally grateful.

He hands over his manuscript and goes. Mahler glances at it, puts it aside. He begins to pace furiously, in a state of great alarm.
He stops, frozen, as if stricken.
The fifth movement of the 'Resurrection' Symphony bursts out, 'In Tempo des Scherzo'.
Blackout.

Little St Michael's Church, 23 February 1897.
The music continues throughout what follows. Bright funnel of light on Mahler, kneeling, looking heavenward. He is transfixed, as if the music is sounding in his head.

38

The light grows to reveal Natalie, in a dress, and Anna. Both wear hats. Siegfried beside them. Father Swider, in his priestly robes, steps into the light.

Father Swider Abrenuntiátis Sátanae?

Mahler Abrenúntio.

Father Swider Et ómnibus opéribus eius?

Mahler Abrenúntio.

Father Swider Et ómnibus pompis eius?

Mahler Abrenúntio.

Father Swider Créditis in Deum Patrem omnipoténtum creatórum caeli et terrae?

Mahler Credo.

Father Swider Créditis in Iesum Christum, Filium eius únicum, Dóminum nostrum, natum ex Maria Vírgine, passum et sepúltum, qui a mórtuis resurréxit et sedet ad déxteram Patris?

Mahler Credo.

Father Swider Créditis in Spiritum Sanctum, sanctam Ecclésiam cathólicam, sanctórum communiónem, remissiónem peccatórum, carnis resurrectiónem et vitam aetérnam?

Mahler Credo.

Father Swider turns away to dip his hand into the font and, as he does so, Mahler's face suddenly contorts as the music of the 'Resurrection' Symphony gives way to the Jewish theme from the third movement of the First Symphony.

*To this music and to the intense agony of Mahler,
Father Swider anoints him:*

Father Swider Gustav, ego te baptizó in nómine Patris,
et Filii, et Spiritus Sancti.

*The light on Mahler alone. He covers his ears with
his hands. Silence. He gazes out, expressionless. He
removes his hands from his ears. The Jewish theme
returns.*
   Lights fade to blackout.
   End of Act One.

Act Two

Vienna. Court Opera, 11 May, 1897.
  In darkness, the Finale of Lohengrin. *It ends.*
Tumultuous applause.
  Intense shaft of light on Mahler on the podium. He
turns and bows. He stands, triumphant.
  Blackout.

Vienna. Café Imperial.
  Morning. Siegfried and Natalie reading newspapers.

Natalie These are wonderful. It's as if he wrote them
himself. Listen to this. *The New Musical Press.*
(*Reads.*) 'Just as there are complete works of art,
Gustav Mahler is a complete conductor. His concern
is for the orchestra, the singers and chorus alike. His
glance, his will, his gestures command and unite the
ensemble of performers. Despite his mobility and
vivacity, each gesture is of such eloquence, each
intention so easily grasped, that singers and orchestra
follow him easily and joyfully, as if they had been
used to them for years.' (*to Siegfried*) He's conquered
them! These are the most glorious reviews I have ever
read.

Siegfried Yes, glorious. Listen to this one. (*Reads.*)
'The Jewification of the Opera is complete. Last night,

Gustav Mahler gave us a very Jewish *Lohengrin*.' And this: 'Last night, Herr Mahler started his Jew boy antics on the podium –' (*Laughs.*) Yes, he's conquered them all right – conquered them – (*He laughs helplessly.*)

Blackout.

A house in the Alserbachstrasse, 1901.
  Night. Mahler, alone, lighting a cigar.
  A young woman enters cautiously. She is Alma Schindler, aged 22, unconventionally beautiful.
  Mahler is suddenly aware of her. He smiles. She glows.

Alma Are you not well?

Mahler I'm perfectly well, thank you, why do you ask?

Alma You left the table so suddenly I thought you'd been taken ill.

Mahler I sometimes need to be alone.

Alma I'll go –

Mahler Don't. Please. Don't.

  Silence. But now a sound, as if in his mind, a mysterious, distant piano: one finger picking out the theme of the Adagietto from the Fifth Symphony.

Alma An enjoyable dinner party, don't you think? Not too many Jews.

Nothing from Mahler.

Don't worry, I know you were born a Jew but you're baptised now and that makes a world of difference.

Mahler Yes, a world of difference.

They stare at each other. The sound of the piano more insistent. Then:

Alma You don't remember me, do you?

The piano stops.

Mahler How could I? We were introduced for the first time tonight. Weren't we?

Alma No.

Mahler We've met before?

Alma Oh, yes.

Mahler When?

Alma Two years ago.

Mahler Where?

Alma At Ausee. I asked for your autograph.

Mahler Did I give it to you?

Alma You sent me a postcard. (*She produces it from her reticule.*) It's dated 5th of July, 1899.

Mahler What did I say?

Alma (*without reading it*) 'Sole genuine signature, protected by law: Gustav Mahler. Beware of imitations.'

Mahler Doesn't sound like me at all.

Alma You don't remember.

Mahler I'm afraid not.

Alma I thought tonight at dinner you stared at me as though you did.

Mahler No. I stared at you because – (*He falters.*)

Alma Because?

Mahler Because I couldn't take my eyes off you.

Silence.

Alma I don't like your First Symphony.

Mahler Thank you.

Alma But I love watching you conduct.

Mahler I'm sorry.

Alma I compose, too.

Mahler I'm sure you do, it's the easiest thing in the world. Tell me about yourself.

Alma Oh, can't you do better than that?

Mahler Can't I do better than what?

Alma Such a trite, drab approach: 'Tell me about yourself.'

Mahler All right, don't tell me about yourself.

Alma My name is Alma Maria Schindler. I am twenty-two years old. My father was Emil Schindler, the finest landscape painter in Europe. So I am the daughter of a great monument. He died nine years

ago. My mother remarried. Her second husband is
also a painter, Carl Moll, but he is not a monument.

Mahler I shall call you Marie. It was my mother's
name.

Alma Please don't. I can't bear to be called Marie.

Mahler Are you married, engaged?

Alma Neither. Nor are you.

Mahler No.

Alma Your sister looks after you, I believe.

Mahler Yes, Justine. But how do you know all this?

Alma Everyone knows everything about you. That's
what being famous means. I expect you love it.

He starts to pace.

Mahler Why don't you like my First Symphony?

Alma Because it's an ear-splitting, nerve-shattering din.

Mahler I can't wait to hear your music, you must
show me something you've written.

Alma With pleasure.

Mahler When?

Alma When what?

Mahler When will you bring me one of your pieces?

Alma When I have something worthwhile.

He stops pacing, gazes at her.

Mahler It can't be soon enough.

Alma The other night I attended a recital of your songs. I didn't like any of them but one I thought particularly dreadful.

Mahler Only one? Which was that?

Alma 'The Drummer Boy.' So morbid and gloomy.

Mahler Yes, it's autobiographical.

He paces again. She watches him.

Alma Do you always storm round rooms like a savage?

Mahler Yes.

Alma I think you're made entirely of oxygen. I'm afraid if I go near you I'll get burned.

He stops pacing.

Mahler Funnily enough, I have the same impression of you.

They stare at each other.

I expect you like ballet music.

Alma Not the stupid ballets you stage.

Mahler Then you have fashionable tastes.

They continue to gaze at each other.

Alma What's it feel like to be the most famous and powerful man in Vienna?

Mahler Why do you ask?

Alma Because I'm interested.

Mahler In me, power or in fame?

Alma All three.

Mahler Yes, I forgot, you collect autographs.

Alma Only the genuine article.

Charged silence.

Mahler Why did you bring that postcard?

Alma Because I knew you'd be here.

Their eyes are locked. Silence.
The first movement (second subject) of the Sixth Symphony.
Lights fade to blackout.

Mahler's apartment in Auenbruggergasse. 1 January 1902.
Afternoon.
Mahler bursts in, dishevelled, in a terrible state. He is weeping.

Mahler Don't follow me, don't come near me, I don't want you to look at me – I'm so ashamed – I don't think – I can bear – to look at you –

After a moment, Alma enters in disarray, her hair loose. She wants to go to him but doesn't.

Alma (*a command*) Don't cry!

Mahler I'm sorry. I'm so sorry.

Alma (*at breaking point*) Please! Don't cry! (*She sucks her thumb.*)

Mahler I'm ashamed, terribly ashamed, I wanted you so much –

He sinks down on a sofa, still crying.

Alma (*in despair*) I don't know how to comfort you –

She sucks her thumb again. He turns to her, holds out his arms. She runs to him and kneels. He holds her close, tightly, desperately.
Now she cries uncontrollably.

Mahler I love you too much –

Alma (*through her tears*) When you carried me to the sofa – when you swung yourself over on me you felt so strong – so vigorous – I – I – then – then – I could feel you lose your strength –

Mahler Don't, please, don't –

Alma No, no, no, it doesn't matter – I'm consumed with longing – nothing else matters – I love every part of you – that's all that matters – I love you – say you love me –

Mahler I love you, Alma, I love you – I wanted so much – to be one with you – I want to lose myself in you – lose myself –

Alma You will – you will – I love you – kiss me – let me feel your tongue – eat me – I want to eat you – (*They kiss.*) Let me kiss every part of you. Every part of you – (*She buries her face in his loins.*)

Blackout.

48

The same. Days later.

Evening. Siegfried with a wrapped package, and Natalie, wearing a dress, but she's made too much effort to appear feminine.

Long silence.

Natalie We always seem to be waiting for him.

Siegfried They probably don't know we're here.

Natalie Of course, they do, the maid will have announced us.

Siegfried Perhaps the maid didn't want to interrupt. (*He chuckles.*)

Natalie I'm told she's had many affairs.

Siegfried I doubt it.

Natalie Why?

Siegfried She's a tease. She is reported to have said she likes great men. She wants to be close to the flame. But up to now she's not been burned.

Natalie How d'you know such a thing?

Siegfried One knows, that's how.

Natalie Have you met her?

Siegfried No, but I know people who have.

Natalie How did you find out they were engaged?

Siegfried I forget now, someone told me.

Natalie Not Gustav.

Siegfried No. Not Gustav.

49

Natalie No. I had to read it in the newspaper. (*suddenly tearful*) He might have told me himself.

Siegfried Great men seldom perform unpleasant tasks themselves.

Natalie She's not our sort, that's why he didn't tell us.

Siegfried No, she's certainly not our sort.

Natalie She's extremely rich.

Siegfried Extremely.

Natalie And the worst kind of anti-Semite.

Siegfried What's the best kind?

Natalie I'm told she just says what she thinks. Men find that very attractive. Apparently. She's taken to wearing her hair loose. So – so vulgar.

Siegfried The rich are often vulgar. And I heard she wears her hair loose because that's the way Gustav likes it. (*Smiles.*) Gustav, you see, has a certain inherited vulgarity. (*He chuckles.*)

Natalie Why didn't he introduce us to her sooner? Why wait until they're engaged? Is he secretly ashamed of her, do you think?

Siegfried He's secretly ashamed of so many things.

Natalie What, what can he possibly be ashamed of?

Siegfried Of not becoming himself. (*He chuckles.*)

Natalie (*controlling tears*) I am filled with such a – such a sense of loss.

Siegfried I know the feeling. And so does he.

Natalie And terrible foreboding. I can't help –

Anna enters looking more magnificent than ever.

Siegfried Anna! What a surprise! And what a pleasure. Welcome back!

Anna Sigi, Natalie.

Siegfried Such a long time since we've met. How long is it?

Anna Months.

Siegfried Congratulations on your success in America. When Vienna's not talking about Mahler, Vienna's talking about you.

Natalie We didn't know you'd be joining us.

Anna I guessed you'd be here because he sent me a card: 'I want my dearest friends to meet my bride.'

Natalie Bride? Bride? He didn't say bride to me, he said fiancée –

Siegfried (*smiling sympathetically*) Dear Natalie.

Natalie, overcome, runs from the room.
Immediately, Siegfried and Anna kiss passionately,
his hands all over her.

Siegfried I love you, I adore you, I want you –

Anna Ssh! Oh God, you're a caveman, that's what you are, a caveman –

Siegfried You were glorious last night – I must have you again – now – now – this minute – I must – now –

Anna (*breaking away, laughing*) Not now, Sigi, and not here, we're in someone else's flat –

Siegfried How can you be so cruel?

Anna How can you be so ridiculous?

Siegfried I hope you're not talking about us. I hope for once you're being uncharacteristically discreet –

Anna Of course I am. No one knows. Not even your wife.

Siegfried I hope you're right. If there's a whisper –

Anna No one knows about us!

Siegfried (*taking hold of her again*) Tonight, please, I implore you, look, I'm salivating; I'll book a room at a country inn –

Natalie returns. Anna and Siegfried break apart and appear innocent.

Natalie Haven't they joined you yet? I apologise. This is such a strain. If they don't come soon, I won't stay –

Mahler enters.

Mahler My dear friends –

They all greet him warmly.

Anna, you're looking more wonderful than ever. I hear you had a great success in America. I hope it didn't harm your voice.

He stares at her as if sending a secret signal.
A moment before she understands.

Anna America harmed nothing but my sleep. I believe Americans only attend the opera so that they can have a party afterwards. I don't think I slept more than two hours a night.

Siegfried Alone, I trust.

All but Natalie laugh.

Mahler And dear, dear Natalie. You're looking so –
so – Alma won't be a moment. We've been – (*He runs
dry; long, awkward pause.*) Well, Sigi, what's the
gossip? Come on, you always know everything.

Siegfried Let's see. Vienna, in this year of their Lord,
1902 –

Alma enters, hair loose, her mood hostile.

Mahler Ah, at last. Let me introduce my dearest
friends, my true family: Alma Schindler, Anna von
Mildenburg

Alma Good evening. Welcome. Gustav talks of you
often. But he made you sound much younger.

Mahler alone laughs.

Anna No, no, I'm getting on. We're about the same
age, aren't we?

Mahler And this is Natalie Bauer-Lechner. To whom
I'm devoted.

Alma Yes, of course. But you disappoint me.

Natalie Do I, oh dear, why?

Alma I thought you'd be dressed as a – quite
differently.

Mahler And Siegfried Lipiner.

Siegfried (*kissing her hand and bowing*) Dear lady.

Alma sits; another very awkward silence.

I've brought you a gift. (*He hands her the package.*)

Alma How kind. Thank you. (*She opens it. A painting.*)

Siegfried It's a copy. Of course.

Alma Of what?

Siegfried Guido Reni. He's my favourite painter.

Alma What on earth does it represent?

Siegfried (*bristling*) It's called 'Madonna of the Rosary' and, surprisingly, represents the Madonna of the Rosary. Guido Reni is one of the great masters of the Italian baroque.

Alma Is he indeed? He seems to be a great master of Italian clutter.

Siegfried Little girl, this is one of the finest examples of his work. It was painted in 1632. This copy was done by one of his pupils. It is very dear to me.

Alma But it's rather sickly, don't you think?

Siegfried No, I do not.

Alma I don't think I like Guido Reni.

Siegfried You had better learn to like him if you want to be considered cultured.

He turns his back on her. Mahler goes to him.

Mahler (*angry*) That was uncalled for. We don't all have to admire what you admire.

Mahler returns to Alma. They whisper and laugh, ignoring the others. They also touch each other a good deal. After a moment:

Siegfried (*to Natalie*) This is monstrous –

Natalie Don't make a scene, please don't make a scene –

Siegfried A scene has already been made.

Anna Look at them. We might as well not be here.

Siegfried We should leave. I'm not used to being treated like this.

Natalie No, no, I can't bear rows, we mustn't row –

Anna He's changed. He's not the same man. And playing such games.

Natalie What d'you mean, games?

Anna He wanted you to think this is the first time he's seen me since my return. But the truth is, the moment I heard about his engagement, I went to his office at the opera, pretended to have hysterics, then pretended to faint. To comfort me, he told me he had lied to her. He told her he hardly knew me and had certainly never – (*Stops.*) When you lie to the one you're supposed to love –

Mahler turns to them.

Mahler Well, Sigi. I asked you what the latest gossip was. He always knows everything that's going on, don't you, Sigi? That's really your métier.

Alma Oh good. Yes, yes, the latest gossip, please, anything and everything, apart from the whispers about you and Fräulein von Mildenburg.

Siegfried (*horrified*) Me and Fräulein von Mildenburg? What d'you mean? This is the first time we've met for – for –

Anna (*cool*) For months.

Alma But the whole town's talking about you.

Siegfried (*to Mahler, alarmed*) Is it?

Mahler Don't let it upset you. It's better to be talked about than not to be talked about.

Alma Gustl's talked about all the time. We both are. It's divine. You've no idea how many people claim to have introduced us, or to have got Gustl the job as Director of the Court Opera. What they can't bear to admit is that Fate engineered our meeting.

Siegfried (*quietly, to Anna*) Poor old Fate, blamed for everything –

Anna laughs quietly.

Alma And as for the Court Opera, he did it himself, didn't you, sweetheart? You did it yourself. Great men need no friends and have no friends.

Siegfried (*a loud whisper, to Anna*) That, I think, is the stupidest remark I've ever heard.

Mahler (*dangerous, to Siegfried*) What did you say?

Alma It doesn't matter, Gustl. Come along, Herr Lipiner. We're waiting. For the latest gossip.

Siegfried I know no gossip.

Silence.

Anna You must be very proud of your great man, Fräulein Schindler.

Alma Very.

Anna And I expect you love his music.

Alma I know very little of it, and the little of it I know I don't like.

Mahler laughs.

Siegfried I suppose you think that's clever, do you, little girl?

Alma No, not clever, just truthful.

Natalie (*softly, to Anna*) I think it's tragic.

Silence.

Anna And when are you to be married?

Mahler The date's not yet fixed. But soon.

Anna Ah, now I understand.

Alma Understand what?

Anna Why you're so on edge, the pair of you. The waiting to get at each other must be agony. (*She laughs.*)

Alma We've already made love.

Mahler (*chuckling*) Almschi –

Alma We waited until we were engaged, of course.

Siegfried Of course –

Alma The first time was on New Year's Day. It was a disaster. The second time was bliss. Pure rapture. As a matter of fact, we were making love just as you arrived. That's why we kept you waiting. Sheer heaven.

Anna swoons.

Mahler Oh, get up, Anna. Stop doing that, it's so tiresome –

Siegfried goes to Anna and helps her.
Dreadful silence.

Natalie And have you chosen the church yet?

Alma I'd like to be married in a field. I don't believe in all that religious nonsense. I don't believe in God. (*Natalie gasps.*) Which is why I suppose I find this painting, Herr Lipiner, rather cloying. What's the artist's name?

Mahler You mustn't say you don't believe in God, Almschi.

Alma Why? It's the truth.

Mahler God is not mocked. You do believe, I know you do believe. You believe in Christ the Saviour.

Alma That's rich coming from you, Gustl.

Siegfried Yes, it's a wonderful spectacle to witness a Jew defending Christ to a Gentile.

Alma (*abruptly*) I have a headache. (*She goes.*)

Siegfried I'm leaving, too.

Mahler Don't. (*Awkward pause.*) She makes me immensely happy. Isn't that the important thing?

Siegfried snorts

She's young. She's embarrassed by strangers. She's shy.

Siegfried turns on Mahler, seething.

Siegfried Whenever I'm told someone's shy, I know there's a monster lurking beneath. And I blame you. You encourage her and show your friends nothing but contempt –

Mahler That's not true, Sigi, what did I do?

Siegfried You're so self-centred you wouldn't notice if she behaved badly or not. Her manners are outrageous, her vulgarity unforgiveable. Fancy not liking Guido Reni. And you take her part. You know why? Not because you're besotted by her, which you obviously are, but because deep down you want to be rid of us.

Mahler I do not –

Siegfried Oh yes, you do. You're part of the new world now, the glittering, powerful, world. Catholic Vienna, that's your new reality, isn't it? We're just objects to you, to be dispensed with at will. Perhaps your future wife alone will satisfy your needs. She knows all the real people and flirts with most of them. You'd better live with her in splendid isolation, untroubled by the likes of us. You're cold, Gustav, profoundly, lastingly, everlastingly cold. You belong now, all right. You've found a home, but I never want to visit it again.

Dangerous silence.

Mahler Show yourselves out.

He goes. Natalie bursts into tears. Siegfried goes to her.

Anna One thing's certain. It won't last. How could one be married to that for more than a week?

Natalie (*controlling tears, with great dignity*) We'll never see him again. I know that. Never. I'm writing a book about him. Whether I ever finish it is in the hands of the Supreme and Eternal Master.

Anna (*smiling at Natalie*) If I've been unkind to you in the past, Natalie, I apologise. You have great dignity. I wish I had it. I think I admire dignity in a human being more than any other quality.

> *She takes Natalie out. Siegfried hesitates for a moment, then collects his Guido Reni. Clutching it, he goes.*
> *Blackout.*

Mahler's study. A few moments later.
Alma seated, very still, sucking her thumb. Mahler enters. Her back is to him.

Mahler They've gone. I asked them to leave.

Alma Thank God for that. What dreadful people. Did you hear him call me 'little girl', not once but twice? (*She sucks her thumb again.*)

Mahler For God's sake, stop sucking your thumb.

Alma Why? What do you want me to suck?

> *Mahler winces.*

Such condescension. The Madonna and the Rosary. So affected. And so arrogant. Typical from a Jew, baptised or not. I think he's the most sterile person I've ever met. How dare he insist I admire Guido Reni in whom I have no interest whatsoever. They're all the same. I refuse to see them again. As for your former mistresses –

Mahler I've told you a hundred times, Anna was not my mistress, that was simply gossip, and as for Natalie, please –

Alma They belittle me so they can have power over you.

Mahler They did not belittle you –

Alma And they're so patronising. I can't bear to be patronised. I am an artist in my own right. I am also a composer and I should be respected, not disparaged.

Silence.

Mahler This should be the happiest time of our lives, why must it be filled with such anxiety and torment?

Alma Because we come from worlds apart.

Silence.

Mahler You won't like what I'm going to say but I'm going to say it nevertheless. You are too used to being flattered. And you've been flattered for your beauty not for your talent and intellect.

She stares at him in disbelief.

I'm sorry but you must face the truth. I love you, Almschi. More than love you, worship you. But if we're to be married, you must stop composing. You have only one profession now: to make me happy.

Alma (*aghast*) What? What did you say? How dare you! How dare you say that to me? I'm just as much of an artist as you are – I'm just as much – how dare you, how dare you ask me to change? I can't change. I won't.

Mahler Then marry someone else.

Alma Why are you punishing me like this?

Mahler I'm not punishing you. I want to live with you for the rest of my life and I'm telling you the only way we can make it possible.

Alma I can't believe you're saying these things –

Mahler I have to protect myself. I have to protect my art. If you were a real artist you'd understand that.

Alma I am a real artist, my music is as good as yours, better –

Mahler I have to protect what I am.

She sobs bitterly but he does not go to her.

I love you. I will never betray you. Never. You're glorious. You've transformed and enriched my life. For the first time in countless years I belong. I belong to you. You were right when you talked of Fate engineering our meeting. But I prefer to believe it was God who willed we should be one. I know that all the mysterious forces beyond our understanding have contrived to bring us together.

Her tears run dry. He stands, watching her. Then:

Alma I hate loving you.

He smiles; she rushes into his arms; they kiss; she holds him tightly.

There are two mes. The good me knows that what you ask is right. The bad one resists with all her strength. The trouble is that, often, I don't know which is the real me. If there is a real me. Sometimes, that second self, vain and bad, demands to be let out. And I can't stop it. And it fills me with shame.

Both are now lost in their own inner worlds.

Mahler I understand. Believe me. I understand the struggle. I understand what it is to be divided. But we have to achieve harmony. In ourselves. And together.

Alma (*stepping back*) But how? How?

> *Silence.*
> *Blackout.*

Music from 'Kindertotenlieder'.
> *Alma appears. She's wheeling a pram. She stops. She stares into space. From somewhere, the sound of a small child playing happily. She glances in the direction of the sound then goes slowly. The music continues.*
> *Blackout.*

The music loud and insistent.
> *Mahler, alone, writing. The music is in his head. He does not look up. He writes. The music continues.*
> *Blackout.*

Sudden silence. Alma, alone. Her face hard and
resentful.
  Knocking on the door.

Mahler's Voice Almschi? Almschi?

  She does not move. The door is tried but is locked.
  The knocking continues. She remains unmoved,
  implacable.
    Blackout.

Café Imperial. A private room. August, 1910.
  Siegfried on a telephone.

Siegfried Dr Singer? Siegfried Lipiner. No, I'm in
perfect health, thank you, but I have a great favour to
ask of you. I will explain the circumstances first, and
ask the favour afterwards. In that way, I know you
won't refuse. (*Chuckles; listens.*) You're very kind. By
chance, I've just met again someone I used to know
very well but haven't seen for more than, my God,
it must be six, seven years. The reunion, so to speak,
occurred in unfortunate circumstances. I was crossing
to the Café Imperial, which is where I am now –
(*Listens.*) Yes, I'm talking to you from a private room.
Unusually for me I was minding my own business
when I saw a small crowd gathered around a figure
who'd collapsed in the street. I went to investigate.
I recognised my friend, deathly pale, and very weak.
She was distressed at seeing me and wanted to run
away – (*Listens.*) Because she was ashamed. She had
no money and hadn't eaten for two days. She's fallen

on hard times and is too proud to admit it. I brought her here, ordered some soup and – (*Listens, laughs.*) Yes, of course, chicken soup. This is the favour I want to ask. She doesn't look at all well. So, could I bring her to your surgery in, say, half an hour? (*Listens.*) Thank you. You're a dear man, Dr Singer.

A knock on the door.

In half an hour. Thank you so much. (*Replaces the receiver; calls.*) Yes?

Natalie enters, her appearance greatly altered. She wears a skirt, but with a tattered male jacket. Her hair is grey and untidy. She is pale. But her dignity is still intact.

Natalie I came to thank you. Now I must go.

Siegfried Sit for a moment. Please.

After hesitating, she sits.

I have a favour to ask. Will you come with me now to visit a friend of mine?

Natalie (*vehemently, distressed*) No! I don't want to see him. No, no, no! Not him! Not him!

Siegfried Who are you talking about?

Natalie You know very well.

Siegfried is puzzled for a moment. Then:

Siegfried Oh! No, no, no, you misunderstand –

Natalie I haven't clapped eyes on him since that dreadful night in his apartment –

Siegfried Nor have I –

Natalie And I never want to clap eyes on him again.

Siegfried He travels back and forth to America.

Natalie America? What's he do in America?

Siegfried What everybody does in America. Makes money. I've heard he plans to go to New York at least once a year.

Natalie Really.

Siegfried Yes. Ever since –

Natalie (*fierce*) What a dreadful, dreadful tragedy. (*Silence.*) Terrible to lose a child. In my own small way, I know what it feels like when one's world collapses.

Nothing from Siegfried.

I had two reasons for living – Gustav Mahler and the diary I kept in which I wrote down every word he uttered. Then I was abandoned. Simply cut adrift. I'm not sure I know exactly what happened after that. I didn't seem to notice that I was becoming – I think the word is 'destitute'.

Siegfried You played the cello, couldn't you have given lessons?

Natalie I had to sell my cello.

Siegfried I wish you'd written to me. I'd have helped. I'll help now –

Natalie No. No charity. Thank you. (*Silence.*) He had everything. The whole world. And overnight –

Silence.

And yet he goes on composing. The little I have I spend on attending concerts to hear his music. I even managed a trip to Prague last year to hear him conduct his Seventh Symphony.

Siegfried He'll overtake Beethoven if he isn't careful.

Natalie And his songs. Such beautiful songs. 'The Drummer Boy.' 'Where the Splendid Trumpets Sound. Heavenly Life.' (*Brief silence.*) And he's still married to that awful woman. I have nightmares about her. I never thought it would last.

Siegfried No one did.

Natalie What can possibly have kept them together?

Siegfried The forces that divide them. (*He laughs; silence.*) It's the same for all of us.

Natalie You've always been too clever for me. But you've changed. You're more subdued than you once were. Why?

He smiles crookedly. Then:

Siegfried My first wife and I divorced. I married again. In the eyes of the Church I was living in sin which was, between you and me, the least of my problems. I was, am, also – divided.

Natalie Divided? I don't understand –

He waves the question away.

Siegfried I went to a psychoanalyst. After two sessions, he said he didn't want to treat me any longer. I asked him why. He said because I knew more about myself than he ever would. That helped. I don't know why but it helped. Perhaps I've become myself. Or not. As the case may be.

Natalie There is one thing I shall never understand.

Siegfried Only one?

Natalie It is difficult for someone as insignificant and as untalented as I am. But explain this to me: how can a great composer be such an indifferent human being?

Siegfried It's often the way. Richard Wagner was exactly the same, only worse. I knew him. Awful, really. Really awful.

Natalie Why is it?

Siegfried Because someone else writes their music. (*Chuckles.*) Natalie, come with me now –

Natalie Where?

Siegfried I want you to see my friend, Dr Singer.

Natalie I can't afford a doctor.

Siegfried But I can. Don't be proud. We go back a long way. It's the least I can do.

Natalie (*stands; a smile*) I wonder if he can cure a broken heart.

Siegfried Yours or mine? (*He laughs.*)

  Blackout.

Leiden, Holland. 26 August 1910.
A park with a bench.
Sigmund Freud, aged 54, smoking a cigar. He is
waiting, patiently. He glances at his watch. As he does
so, Mahler enters. He's aged 50 now and is ill. He is
out of breath.

Mahler Dr Freud –

Freud rises and they shake hands.

Freud Dr Mahler. Good. At last. I was fully expecting
another one of your telegrams cancelling our meeting.

Nothing from Mahler.

Usually, I do not consult when I'm on holiday but,
although I know nothing about music, I could not
refuse a man of your reputation and worth.

Mahler Thank you. I apologise if I've inconvenienced
you. The two previous appointments I made and then
cancelled were because – (*He runs dry.*)

Freud I cannot pretend not to be intrigued. We live,
what, ten minutes walk away from each other in
Vienna? Yet you waited for me to take a holiday
abroad before making an appointment. Which you
twice cancelled. In all I received five telegrams from
you. Quite a collection. Two making appointments,
two cancelling them, and one making another
appointment. Which you have kept. And so here we
are. Leiden is as good a place to talk as any.

He sits. Mahler stands awkwardly for a moment
and then sits beside him.

Mahler You helped my young colleague Bruno Walter.
I was most impressed. The pain in his arm was really

excruciating. He simply couldn't conduct. And he told me that you didn't question him about sexual aberrations in infancy, or talk about the Oedipus complex, which is what he expected, but you just briefly examined his arm, then told him to take a holiday in Sicily. You ordered him, I believe, to leave that very evening and to forget all about his arm and the opera, and do nothing for a few weeks but use his eyes.

Nothing from Freud.

For people like us, taking a rest is only possible when we are ill.

Freud Are you ill, Dr Mahler?

Mahler rises, paces, sits again but now turned away from Freud.

Mahler I have recently been diagnosed as having a weak heart, but that's not why I –

Long silence.

Freud I must warn you that in the short time available to us this afternoon, I cannot possibly effect anything like a cure. At best, I may be able to guide you on the right path, but little more than that.

Silence.

Mahler I have become impotent.

Silence.

My wife is having an affair. A young man. An architect.

Silence.

In the last three years, my entire life has collapsed. First, there was a vicious anti-Semitic press campaign against me and I was forced to resign from the Court Opera. Then – (*Fights tears.*) I had two children. Daughters. But the elder one, my beautiful little Maria, died of diphtheria. Not yet five years old. We called her Putzi – (*Cries, recovers.*) Such a beautiful, loving child. That same month, July 1907, the doctors found I had this serious heart complaint.

Silence.

I'm lost to the world.

Silence.

I cannot rid myself of the feeling that I'm being punished.

Freud By whom?

Silence.

Mahler Jehovah.

Freud Why should Jehovah want to punish you?

Mahler Do you believe in God, Dr Freud?

Freud (*as if he hasn't heard the question*) Does the loss of your libido extend to your creativity? Has your music suffered, has your creative energy diminished?

Mahler rises and begins to pace.

Mahler No, no, no, not at all. That's the extraordinary thing. The music pours out of me. It's a struggle, of course, but it pours out of me because in my music –

He falls silent but continues to pace. Freud watches him closely.

Freud Dr Mahler, is the problem with your leg congenital?

Mahler stops pacing.

Mahler My leg?

Freud You limp. Were you born with one leg shorter than the other?

Mahler There's nothing wrong with my leg.

Freud Then why do you limp?

Mahler I don't limp –

Freud Well, you walk in the most curious way. You change rhythm –

Mahler I've always walked like this. Funnily enough, my mother limped. She was born with a malformation –

Silence.

She was a beautiful person. She had a hard, terrible life. She bore my father thirteen children. Only four of us survived infancy. He treated her appallingly. Beat her. When he was drunk. Which was often. I couldn't bear it. (*a sudden realisation*) I see! You're suggesting that the way I walk is in some way related to my mother's misfortune. Am I right?

Freud looks at him in total surprise.

Freud Have you been psychoanalysed before?

Mahler No, never.

Freud Well, well. I've not known anyone understand the process so quickly. Amazing. Yes, I think you walk in the way you do to offer your mother sympathy.

Mahler, beaming, sits beside Freud.

Mahler Really? But I'm finding this most enjoyable.
And there's something else. When I was talking about
my parents a moment ago, a memory darted into my
mind that explains something very important to me.
It was the memory of an awful episode between them.
My father was particularly brutal. I couldn't bear it.
I rushed out of the house. At that precise moment, in
the street, a hurdy-gurdy was grinding out 'Ach, Du
lieber Augustin' – (*He hums the tune.*) Of course!
That must explain it.

Freud I'm not sure I follow.

Mahler I understand now why my music is prevented
from achieving the highest rank. It's because the
noblest passages, the ones inspired by the most
profound emotions, are spoilt by the intrusion of
commonplace tunes, trite, vulgar little tunes; I can't
keep them out. I've never said this to anyone else. I
can only confess it to you. Do you understand? When
I heard 'Ach, Du lieber Augustin' after that terrible
row, the collision of high tragedy and what is
ordinary, amusing, mundane, must have been
inextricably fixed in my mind. Am I right?

Freud Are you sure you haven't been psychoanalysed
before?

Mahler And another thing. Critics, mostly anti-Semitic
critics, of course, or Jews wanting to claim me as their
own, they say my music is full of Jewish tunes. It's
rubbish. Occasionally, there's a lilting wedding dance
or an evocative rhythm or a – but to point to a few
bars in all the music I have written and say I am
haunted by –

Silence; he is lost.

I have written more funeral marches than any other composer who has ever lived.

Silence.

I think about death constantly.

Silence.

I am terrified of death.

Silence.

I compose in a hut. I start. When I look up, the hours have vanished. My work demolishes time. I was young a moment ago. And now I am not.

Silence.

I'm not long for this world.

Silence.

I cannot imagine this world without me in it.

Freud The arrogance of consciousness.

Mahler The arrogance of consciousness. Yes, I see. You don't believe in God.

Silence.

There is a division between who I am, who I am and who I am. As a conductor, as director of the opera, as a performer, I am certain of everything. I have no doubts whatsoever. But as a human being I am riddled with doubt. And as a composer, I describe the chaos, the confusion and uncertainty of life, my life, your life, all life. And the beauty, too, love, nature, the fleeting rays of happiness. But mostly uncertainty. And the descent into destruction. That's why people resist my music. Our world is disintegrating and they can't face it. God only knows what lies in store for us. It's a vision of a new, horrifying universe. That's also why my music is so unpredictable, because life is totally unpredictable, savage, cruel. To be human is to be uncertain. Have you ever heard my music?

Freud (*after hesitating*) No –

Mahler Listen to it. It may help you understand the world we live in.

Freud is a little taken aback.

Is there a cure for impotence?

Silence.

I worship my wife. But I'm afraid. I am so much older than she is.

Silence.

We have known great happiness together.

Silence.

But not recently. She locked her bedroom door.

Silence.

A younger man.

Silence.

The first time I tried to make love to her, I failed. The memory never leaves me.

Freud Your wife, if I am correct, had a remarkable father, Emil Schindler.

Mahler Yes, she loved him deeply.

Freud Then perhaps it is your age which is what precisely attracts her to you. Don't be anxious. You loved your mother and you look for her in every woman. It's not uncommon. And may, in your case, relate to a Holy Mary complex.

Mahler stares at him blankly. Silence.

Mahler My worst nightmare is now a reality. I've always been terrified of becoming a spiritual wanderer, the Eternal Jew; it's a dream I had as a child, his cloak billowing in a howling wind, offering me a gnarled staff topped by a golden cross. And that's what I've become, sailing the ocean back and forth to the new world, and finding nothing but sterility, yes, and impotence. There will be only one resting place for me, one true, still centre. Oblivion.

Silence.

I am being punished.

Freud Tell me why you think you're being punished.

Mahler You don't believe in God, you won't understand.

Freud God is an illusion, Dr Mahler.

Mahler Oh, really? Well, if that's what you believe, so be it. Then the composing of music is also an illusion, all art is an illusion, because I tell you of my own knowledge that creation comes not from within but from without. From God! But you will probably say this is also an illusion. Or even neurotic. Ridiculous. Forgive me for saying so, but about the creative process you understand absolutely nothing.

Freud (*unprovoked, calm*) The conviction that one is being punished relies on a system of beliefs that is directly related to all you have just said.

Mahler Whether illusory or not, the conviction is real.

Freud (*delighted*) Precisely, Dr Mahler. You are indeed very quick. So, if you carry the conviction that you're being punished, you must also, logically, carry the conviction that you've committed a crime. You can't believe you're being punished for no reason whatsoever.

Silence.

Mahler Were you ever tempted to convert?

Freud I avoided it. As one would a seduction.

Mahler I did not. There was no other way.

Freud rises and starts to walk. Mahler walks with him. They stop, walk, stop. Mahler has to catch his breath from time to time.

Freud I am in the process of considering a work on religious psychopathology, so what I am going to tell you must be in the strictest confidence. I have many enemies and it is best they are kept in the dark until I am ready to plunge them into light. (*He pauses, relights his cigar.*) All religion is an illusion, Dr Mahler. All religion suppresses the universal essence of humanity. But being a Jew has nothing to do with religious belief. Being a Jew is to possess a common mental construction, radical rather than religious. Which is why, in your case, for example, your conversion of convenience, as one might call it, has not, cannot change your essential Jewishness, which is the inheritance of all the obstinacy, defiance and

77

passion with which our ancestors defended their temple. In your case, your conversion was essentially dishonest. The society in which you lived unfairly demanded that you deny your origins and beliefs in order to rise through its ranks. And you succumbed to what must have seemed to you an intolerable pressure, as great as though you were being raped. Your conversion was psychopathological, a neurotic impulse bordering on the hysterical. Hysterical, because you, like so many other patients of this kind, were made to feel ashamed of being a Jew, then ashamed of being ashamed, and as a result reacted to this mass suggestion of your unjust society and allowed it to seduce you. But the common mental construction of the Jews is immutable and that is why you suffer guilt. Please do not repeat what I have just said.

Mahler looks at him blankly. Freud sits. So does Mahler. After a moment:

Mahler I believe in one God. I believe all men and women are spiritual beings. I believe that death is not an end but a beginning. I believe in the life hereafter. And I do not believe any of these things.

Silence.

Freud Do you know my book *Jokes and their Relation to the Unconscious?*

Mahler No.

Freud takes out a notebook and pages through it.

Freud Jokes, especially Jewish jokes, have, like dreams, deep significance, and are often helpful in understanding the precise world with which they are concerned.

Mahler I despise Jewish jokes.

Freud (*unperturbed*) Here are two that might be of interest to you. And may help. (*Pages through his notebook, finds a page, reads.*) Two poor Jews are passing St Peter's in Rome. They see a sign offering any Jew who converts to Roman Catholicism one million lire. The first Jew decides to enter the Cathedral. After a suitable lapse of time, he emerges. His companion asks him if he has been converted. The first Jew says he has. The second Jew asks if they paid him the one million lire. Says the other, 'That's the trouble with you Jews, all you think about is money.'

   Silence; nothing from Mahler.

The point here is, Dr Mahler, that the converted Jew instantly takes on the attitude and mentality of his new identity for which – and this is most important – he has been handsomely paid but –

   He looks at Mahler, who is staring into space;
   Freud finds another page.

How about this one? A Jew visits his doctor. He tells the doctor he is impotent. 'I am unable to make love to my wife,' he says. The doctor thinks for a moment, then says, 'I suggest you try making love to your maid.' 'No, no,' says the Jew, 'with the maid I'm not impotent.'

   A momentary silence, then Mahler bursts into
   helpless laughter in which Freud joins.

Mahler 'With the maid I'm not impotent.'

Freud Good, eh? 'With the maid I'm not impotent.' You clearly see the point –

The two men laugh until their laughter runs dry. Mahler suddenly stands.

Mahler I don't know how to thank you, Dr Freud.

Freud looks at him with amazement and then concern.

Sympathy for my mother. That's so helpful. So beautiful. of course. And 'Ach, Du lieber Augustin', wonderful. Here's another thing. My mother's name was Marie. My wife's second name is Marie. Don't you find that extraordinary? That's your Oedipus complex in one bar, four-four time, C major. It's not Holy Mary, Dr Freud, it's all God the Father, you see! God the Father! (*He shakes Freud's hand warmly, starts to go, then returns, catches his breath.*) Listen to my music. It will help you understand the world more profoundly than you do. Goodbye.

He goes. Freud watches him, mystified. Then he turns the pages of his notebook, reads, chuckles, turns to another page, reads, laughs out long and loud.
Blackout.

The sound of a tenor coming to the end of 'Der Tambourg' sell' ('The Drummer Boy') from Des Knaben Wunderhorn, *to a piano accompaniment.*

New York. Rehearsal room, January 1911.
   The song ends. Light on Mahler seated before a music stand with music. He turns to the 'singer' (the audience).

Mahler Thank you, Mr Fielding. You sing beautifully. As a matter of fact, you sing too beautifully. No, no, don't interrupt me, just listen to what I have to say. You sing every note perfectly – except, please remember, my quavers are longer than anybody else's quavers – yes, you sing perfectly but you don't seem to understand the song at all. Not at all. And if you don't understand it, how can we expect your fellow Americans to understand it? You could be singing scales for all the feeling you give it. Let me see if I can make clear to you what this song is about because it's very important to me. You must take what I say into yourself, so that the next time you sing it, your voice may, just may, be infused with the true feeling and meaning of the words. The words, Mr Fielding, came first. The words are what I set to music. So. Good. 'The Drummer Boy.' No, no, don't look at the music, just look at me because I am not going to stick strictly to what's written but I am going to imbue you with the feeling of the song. 'The Drummer Boy.' Remember, he is being led to the gallows for an unnamed crime.

   The song sounds distantly.

Yes, an unnamed crime.

   Poor little drummer boy that I am!
   They are dragging me out of my prison cell.
   If only I'd remained a drummer boy,
   I'd never have been in this prison cell.

   Becoming more and more lost.

Oh, Gallows! Up there is my final resting place.
Oh, Gallows! The sight of you chills me because
    I know I belong to you.
When the soldiers march by,
They'll have nothing to do with me.

When they ask who I was,
I cry out to them,
'I was the drummer boy of the First Company!'
Goodnight, goodnight, to all I have loved,
(*Lost now.*) Nature, music, fame, family, friends.

Such shame.

Goodnight, you officers, corporals and musketeers.
My comrades pass and avert their eyes,
I cry with a clear voice,
'I take my leave of you!
Good night! Good night!'

The song finishes. Mahler stares into space, forlorn.
    Lights fade to blackout.

Vienna, Löw Sanatorium. 18 May 1911
    The Adagietto from the Fifth Symphony. Dim light.
Mahler in bed. He is dying. Alma, who cannot hear
the music, is now in her mid-thirties and tired. She sits
at his bedside, opening envelopes and reading letters.
After a moment:

Mahler This is yours, Almschi. This is my love for
you. I heard it the first time I saw you – no, the
second time – (*He falls silent.*)

Siegfried enters. He carries a batch of envelopes.
Alma sees him and gasps.

Alma Who let you in?

Siegfried A nun.

Alma I gave strict instructions –

Siegfried She asked me to give you these. (*He hands over the envelopes.*)

Alma I'd like you to leave.

Siegfried When I've said goodbye.

He goes to the bedside while Alma starts to open the new batch of envelopes.

Gustav?

Mahler opens his eyes.

Mahler Mozart, little Mozart –

Siegfried I'm afraid not. It's only me. Siegfried Lipiner.

Mahler Who?

Siegfried It doesn't matter. An old friend. I didn't know what to bring you so I didn't bring you anything. I'm a very bad hospital visitor. I never know what to say, except, 'How are you?' which in the circumstances never seems appropriate. Or I tell the patient the most depressing news. But I promise to try a different approach today. (*Leans close to him; cheerfully.*) I bring you greetings from Anna von Mildenburg, Bruno Walter and Natalie. They all say, 'Get well immediately.'

Brief silence.

Natalie's had such a bad time –

He stops himself; Alma suddenly laughs at something she reads.

Has he asked for a priest?

Alma Certainly not.

Siegfried I'll take my leave. (*He leans over and kisses Mahler on the brow. He bows to Alma and leaves quickly.*)

Alma What effrontery. Turning up like that, slimy, obsequious, worming his way in here. At least he didn't call me little girl. (*She holds up the letter that made her laugh.*) Aren't people extraordinary! Gustl, do you know what I have here? A bill. Yes, a bill for three hundred crowns. From Professor Doctor Sigmund Freud for a consultation conducted in Leiden, Holland last year. What a time to send a bill. But typical.

Mahler I should have sent him a bill.

Silence.

Alma Three hundred crowns. Well, I suppose it was worth it. It seemed to do the trick.

Silence. The Adagietto again, but very distant now.

Mahler Almschi, oh my Almschi –

She goes to him, mops his brow. She sits, gazing at him.

Alma They're already weeping crocodile tears for you. All wailing for the passing of the great age of opera under Mahler. His like will never be seen again. You know who says these things? The people who drove you out of Vienna, turned you into a wanderer.

Mahler I'm so – I'm so – terribly ashamed –

Alma Don't, Gustl. We were both to blame. You just as much as me. You deliberately stifled my gifts because you thought yours were superior. And I've never been sure that they were. Fancy telling me that I had only one duty and that was to make you happy. I've resented that all my life.

Silence.

Our worlds never really met.

Silence.

You punished me because I was all that you loved and despised.

Silence.

The bad in me loved the bad in you. And still does.

Silence.

Writing songs about the death of children. I begged you not to. And you were the one who said God is not mocked. You'd think that a Jew would understand that. But no, not you. You wrote those songs and two years later our little Maria –

She controls tears. Silence.

We were happy for so short a time.

Silence.

Shall I send for a priest? Or a rabbi?

Mahler Almschi? Almschi?

Alma I'm here.

Silence.

Mahler My time will come.

He closes his eyes, now close to death. She watches him.

The theme from the last movement of the Ninth Symphony erupts.

Sudden yellowish light on a cloaked figure.

great wind. A swirling mist.

The figure could be Father Swider or Sigmund Freud or the Eternal Jew. And the cloak billows, making him hunchbacked.

Alma neither sees the figure nor hears the wind. She sits watching Mahler anxiously.

The figure holds out a twisted staff towards Mahler, but a plain staff without a cross, unadorned and undecorated.

The music continues and then abruptly stops.

Blackout.

The End.